THIS LAND CALLED AMERICA: **MARYLAND**

CREATIVE EDUCATION

Published by Creative Education
P.O. Box 227, Mankato, Minnesota 56002
Creative Education is an imprint of The Creative Company
www.thecreativecompany.us

Book and cover design by Blue Design (www.bluedes.com)
Art direction by Rita Marshall
Printed in the United States of America

Photographs by Alamy (INTERFOTO Pressebildagentur), Corbis (Low-
ell Georgia, Robert Llewllyn/zefa, Richard T. Nowitz, Paul A. Souders,
Tim Tadder), Getty Images (Altrendo Images, Skip Brown, Skip Brown/
National Geographic, Jerry Driendl, Tim Fitzharris, Henry Horenstein,
Kean Collection, Frederic Lewis, MPI, Greg Pease, Medford Taylor, Time
Life Pictures/Mansell/Time Life Pictures, Michael Townsend, Tom
Vezo, Mark Wilson)

Library of Congress Cataloging-in-Publication Data
Wimmer, Teresa.
Maryland / by Teresa Wimmer.
p. cm. — (This land called America)
Includes bibliographical references and index.
ISBN 978-1-58341-645-7
1. Maryland—Juvenile literature. I. Title. II. Series.
F181.3.W56 2008
975.2—dc22   2007015019

First Edition
9 8 7 6 5 4 3 2 1

OR MAP OF 1826.
DS HISTORY OF THE UNITED STATES.

This Land Called America

MARYLAND

Teresa Wimmer

Maryland

TERESA WIMMER

SUNLIGHT GLISTENS OFF THE WATERS OF CHESAPEAKE BAY. CHILDREN RUN ALONG THE WARM, SANDY BEACH. SOME OF THEM WATCH A FISHING BOAT SET OUT TO SEA. THEY WATCH AS THE FISHERMEN TOSS OUT A BIG NET. WHEN THE NET IS PULLED UP, MANY OYSTERS AND CLAMS ARE INSIDE. SEAGULLS AND EGRETS HUNT FOR FISH NEAR THE SHORE. SOMETIMES, THE GULLS SWOOP DOWN FROM THE SKY TO SCOOP A FISH OUT OF THE WATER. IN THE RESTAURANTS THAT LINE THE BEACH, PEOPLE PULL APART CRAB LEGS, AND THE BUTTERY JUICE RUNS DOWN THEIR CHINS. IN THE OCEANIC STATE OF MARYLAND, A GOOD SEAFOOD MEAL IS NEVER HARD TO FIND.

YEAR

1572 Spanish explorer Pedro Menéndez de Avilés becomes the first European to sail into Chesapeake Bay.

EVENT

Baltimore and the Bay

Hundreds of years ago, many Algonquin Indian tribes called Maryland home. On the western side lived the peaceful Piscataway and Powhatan tribes. The Susquehannocks lived in the north. Sometimes, the Susquehannocks attacked their peaceful neighbors and tried to take their land.

C.Smith taketh the King of Pamavnkee prifoner 1608

The area provided the Indians with plenty of food. Men hunted and trapped bears, deer, woodland buffalo, and wild turkeys. The women grew corn, beans, and squash. They gathered clams and oysters from Chesapeake Bay and nuts and strawberries from the woods. The Indians lived in huts made of tree branches and bark.

In the 1500s, Spanish and Italian men explored Chesapeake Bay, but they did not stay. An English captain named John Smith traveled from Virginia (Maryland's neighbor to the south) into Chesapeake Bay in 1608. After he told other Virginians about Maryland's rich farmland and friendly Indians

When he first traveled into Maryland, Captain John Smith (above, right) appreciated the natural beauty of Chesapeake Bay and its islands (opposite).

YEAR

1608 Captain John Smith, an English soldier and sailor, explores Chesapeake Bay.

EVENT

Lord Baltimore died shortly before he could carry out his vision of founding a colony.

with whom they could trade, many people decided to move north to Maryland.

Another Englishman named Lord Baltimore wanted to found a colony in Maryland. He wanted a place where people of all religions could live together peacefully. His son Cecil went to Maryland in 1633. Cecil, along with 150 people, founded the first permanent settlement, St. Mary's, in Maryland. Maryland's largest city, Baltimore, was later named after the pioneering Lord Baltimore.

Most of the Indian tribes in Maryland welcomed the new settlers. They traded furs and weapons with them. They taught them how to grow crops such as beans and corn. The settlers hunted in the woods. They also planted wheat and tobacco in the good soil.

Tobacco leaves are hung in barns to dry so that they can then be turned into cigars and other products.

Tobacco made many planters rich. Most farmers lived in small, wooden shacks. But some of the tobacco farmers built huge homes called plantations on several acres of land. They needed many men to work their land. Farmers brought in slaves from Africa to work the land and harvest the tobacco.

Soon, more and more people came to Maryland. They brought diseases with them such as smallpox. The Indian tribes were not used to these diseases, and many of the natives died. The rest were eventually pushed west by newcomers. The last of the Susquehannocks were killed by a mob in 1763.

YEAR

1633   Cecil Calvert (Lord Baltimore II) arrives from England and takes possession of Maryland.

EVENT

General George B. McClellan's costly victory at Antietam protected Maryland from further invasion.

In 1775, the U.S. and England began fighting the Revolutionary War. Twenty-three thousand Marylanders fought in the war. During one 1776 battle, Marylanders fought off British troops, or "held the line," so that other American troops could reach safety. Three years after becoming a state, in 1791, Maryland made another sacrifice. It gave up some of its land along the Potomac River so the new United States' capital, Washington, D.C., could be built there.

During the American Civil War of 1861–1865, many battles were fought in Maryland. The bloodiest single-day battle in American history was the Battle of Antietam near Sharpsburg, Maryland. More than 23,000 soldiers were killed or wounded there. The battle spurred President Abraham Lincoln to free all of the slaves in the South in January 1863.

By the late 1800s, many people from Ireland, Germany, Russia, Poland, and Italy had come to Maryland. They worked in the factories and in flour, lumber, and textile mills. They also farmed the land. Many of them came for the freedom and better life that Maryland offered. Because of all the people who came, Maryland's towns and cities grew and prospered.

The Battle of Antietam, which occurred on September 17, 1862, was the first battle in a Northern state.

YEAR

1727 The first newspaper in the southern colonies, the *Maryland Gazette*, is founded.

EVENT

Mountains, Apples, and Horses

MARYLAND IS THE NINTH-SMALLEST STATE IN AMERICA. TO THE WEST, IT IS BORDERED BY WEST VIRGINIA. TO THE SOUTH ARE VIRGINIA AND THE DISTRICT OF COLUMBIA. ITS NORTHERN NEIGHBOR IS PENNSYLVANIA, AND ITS EASTERN NEIGHBOR IS DELAWARE. CHESAPEAKE BAY SEPARATES MARYLAND'S EASTERN SHORE FROM THE REST OF THE STATE.

Western Maryland is covered with mountains and forests. The Appalachians and the Allegheny Mountains span much of the area. The state's highest point, Backbone Mountain, is in the Allegheny Mountains. It rises to 3,360 feet (1,024 m).

The land east of the Alleghenys has many green valleys and hills. The soil is excellent for growing grain and for apple orchards. People mine marble, limestone, clay, and coal from the hills. Maryland marble was used to make the Washington Monument in Washington, D.C.

In north-central Maryland, beyond Hagerstown, lie the heavily wooded Blue Ridge Mountains. The mountains were named for the blue haze that seems to hang above them. Past the Blue Ridge Mountains, the land slopes downward into small hills called the Piedmont Plateau. Many farms growing wheat, corn, oats, and beans dot the landscape. Some farmers there raise broiler chickens to sell. Horse farms are also common, as horse racing is a popular sport in Maryland.

Close by Maryland's section of the Blue Ridge Mountains (opposite) are wheat fields and pastures for horses (above).

YEAR

1783

Annapolis becomes the temporary capital of the newly formed United States.

EVENT

- 13 -

The Piedmont Plateau comes to a sudden end at a point called the Fall Line. There, the rivers and streams that wandered through the Piedmont's hills seem to fall off a ledge. Many waterfalls form there. One of the biggest waterfalls is Great Falls on the Potomac River. Baltimore was built at the Fall Line because ships could not go past that point. The Fall Line marks the start of the Atlantic Coastal Plain.

More than half of Maryland sits on the Atlantic Coastal Plain. The Chesapeake Bay divides the Plain into the Eastern Shore and the Western Shore. The Eastern Shore has flat, marshy wetlands with tall grasses. Many birds such as herons and

The Potomac River's Great Falls makes for an exciting whitewater rafting experience for kayakers (opposite) but a challenging experience for a heron looking for dinner (above).

The country's first telegraph line begins operating between Baltimore and Washington, D.C.

EVENT

Chesapeake Bay, at 193 miles (311 km) long and 3 to 25 miles (5–40 km) wide, is home to many islands and harbors.

People who fish for blue crabs in Chesapeake Bay use large, square traps called crab pots.

Chesapeake Bay harbor

terns live in the wetlands. Cypress trees grow there, too. Until a thunderstorm toppled it in 2002, the oldest tree in Maryland was the Wye Oak. It was more than 450 years old.

Many of Maryland's rivers, such as the Susquehanna, were named after Indian tribes. The rivers are home to many kinds of fish, birds, and ducks. The Youghiogheny River is known as Maryland's first "Wild River" because some endangered species that cannot live anywhere else in the world can survive there.

Assateague Island lies off the eastern coast of Maryland. Herds of wild horses roam the island. They eat marsh grass and drink from the freshwater ponds. Legend has it that, long ago, Spanish ships carrying horses sank off the coast of the island. The horses that escaped were stranded, and their descendents are the horses that live on Assateague today.

Perhaps Maryland's most treasured resource is Chesapeake Bay. Its waters provide seemingly endless supplies of fish, clams, crabs, and oysters. In recent years, rivers have carried dirty runoff from chicken farms into Chesapeake Bay. The Bay started to become polluted and too unhealthy for people and animals to enjoy. But Marylanders have worked hard to clean up the Bay. People and shellfish alike can once again be safe in its waters.

YEAR

1845   The U.S. Naval Academy opens in Annapolis on a 10-acre (4 ha) army site named Fort Severn.

EVENT

- 17 -

From Sea to Shore

TODAY, MANY DIFFERENT PEOPLE SHARE MARYLAND'S SPACE. A FEW THOUSAND NATIVE AMERICANS STILL LIVE THERE, BUT THE MAJORITY OF PEOPLE IN MARYLAND ARE WHITE. AFRICAN AMERICANS MAKE UP 29 PERCENT OF THE TOTAL POPULATION. IN PRINCE GEORGES COUNTY, JUST OUTSIDE WASHINGTON, D.C., MORE THAN HALF OF THE PEOPLE ARE AFRICAN AMERICAN. MANY OWN BUSINESSES OR WORK IN POLITICS AND LAW IN THE CAPITAL CITY.

One famous African American from Maryland was Harriet
Tubman. She was born a slave in Dorchester County around 1820
but gained her freedom by running away to the North. In the years
before the Civil War, Tubman helped more than 300 slaves from
the South reach freedom in the North. The route of safe houses
they followed was known as the Underground Railroad.

In the 1800s, immigrants from Ireland, Poland, Italy, and
other European countries arrived in Maryland. Many came
to build the Chesapeake and Ohio Canal. The canal links
Washington, D.C., with Cumberland in western Maryland.
Others worked in coal mines. Both of these tasks involved
putting in long hours and backbreaking work.

*Harriet Tubman (above)
was born in a county
directly across the Bay
from the northernmost
cypress swamp in the
U.S. (opposite).*

As Francis Scott Key watched the attack on Ft. McHenry (above), he wrote the poem (opposite) that would become "The Star Spangled Banner."

Nearly half of Maryland's residents live in the Baltimore area. Another third live just outside Washington, D.C. When immigrants first came to Baltimore, they liked to live close to people from their native countries. In their own ethnic neighborhoods, people could shop for familiar foods and speak the language they knew. Baltimore has kept many of its original neighborhoods intact.

Baltimore's harbor has inspired many people. During the War of 1812, the British attacked Fort McHenry in the Battle of Baltimore. Attorney Francis Scott Key, who was in the harbor negotiating with the British for the release of a prisoner, witnessed the attack. For the entire night, he watched bombs rain down on the fort until smoke blackened the air. The next morning, relieved to see the American flag still waving above the fort, Key wrote a poem called "The Defense of Fort McHenry." It was later renamed "The Star Spangled Banner" and became the U.S.'s national anthem.

YEAR

1876　Johns Hopkins University opens in Baltimore, employing only five teachers its first year.

EVENT

- *20* -

O say can you see ~~through~~ by the dawn's early light
What so proudly we hail'd at the twilight's last gleaming,
Whose broad stripes & bright stars through the perilous flight
O'er the ramparts we watch'd, were so gallantly streaming?
And the rocket's red glare, the bomb bursting in air
Gave proof through the night that our flag was still there
O say does that star spangled banner yet wave
O'er the land of the free & the home of the brave?

On the shore dimly seen through the mists of the deep,
Where the foe's haughty host in dread silence reposes,
What is that which the breeze, o'er the towering steep,
As it fitfully blows half conceals, half discloses?
Now it catches the gleam of the morning's first beam,
In full glory reflected now shines in the stream,
'Tis the star-spangled banner — O long may it wave
O'er the land of the free & the home of the brave!

And where is that band who so vauntingly swore,
That the havoc of war & the battle's confusion
A home & a Country should leave us no more?
~~Their~~ Their blood has wash'd out their foul footsteps pollution
No refuge could save the hireling & slave
From the terror of flight or the gloom of the grave,
And the star-spangled banner in triumph doth wave
O'er the land of the free & the home of the brave.

O thus be it ever when freemen shall stand
Between their lov'd home & the war's desolation!
Blest with vict'ry & peace may the heav'n rescued land
Praise the power that hath made & preserv'd us a nation!
Then conquer we must when our cause it is just,
And this be our motto — "In God is our trust"
And the star-spangled banner in triumph shall wave
O'er the land of the free & the home of the brave.

Today, Maryland is known as a high-tech center. Electronics companies employ many people. The Goddard Space Flight Center has become a leader in the aerospace industry. Many Marylanders also work at Johns Hopkins University or Johns Hopkins Hospital, or on military bases.

More people live in Maryland's cities than on farms. But farming is still important to the state. Farmers raise dairy cattle and broiler chickens. They grow grains such as wheat and corn. Tobacco is still grown there, but smoking has become less popular over time. Tobacco farmers are not as rich today as they once were.

The wheat fields (opposite) of rural Maryland provide a sharp contrast to the lights and busy atmosphere of Baltimore (above).

YEAR

1904 The Great Baltimore Fire burns much of the city, causing $125 million in damage.

EVENT

People on the Eastern Shore sometimes consider themselves separate from the rest of Maryland. Until the Chesapeake Bay Bridge was finished in 1952, it was almost impossible to get from the Western to the Eastern Shore. Eastern Shore residents felt so cut off that they even tried to become a new state!

The Eastern Shore is home to many watermen. Watermen make their living off of Chesapeake Bay. They catch oysters, crabs, fish, and clams. They use boats called skipjacks that are powered by wind. Sometimes the watermen get caught in high winds and storms. Their work is dangerous but exciting.

Using their skipjacks (opposite), fishermen in Chesapeake Bay can catch large quantities of clams (above), as well as many other sea creatures.

YEAR
1952
EVENT

The Chesapeake Bay Bridge opens, spanning the 4.3 miles (7 km) between Maryland's Eastern and Western Shores.

Maryland's Treasures

BECAUSE OF ITS CLEAR WATERS AND MAJESTIC MOUNTAINS, WESTERN MARYLAND IS SOMETIMES CALLED THE "SWITZERLAND OF AMERICA." THE STATE'S LARGEST FRESHWATER LAKE IS THERE. IT IS CALLED DEEP CREEK LAKE. IN THE 1920S, A HYDROELECTRIC CORPORATION DREW WATER FROM NEARBY STREAMS TO MAKE THE LAKE. PEOPLE AND ANIMALS ONCE LIVED WHERE THE LAKE IS NOW.

Now, people enjoy skiing, horseback riding, and going on helicopter rides around the lake. Some people even scuba dive to the bottom. They look for things that belonged to the people who used to live there.

People who like to discover the past also enjoy Calvert Cliffs State Park. The tall cliffs were formed more than 10 million years ago when southern Maryland was covered by a warm sea. Over time, the sea moved back. The cliffs were once the seafloor. Today, people can dig in the sand near the cliffs for shells, shark teeth, and bits of coral.

Each May, the Pimlico Race Course in Baltimore hosts the Preakness Stakes. This race is part of an important three-race series in horse racing called the Triple Crown. Nearly 100,000 people come to watch the 1 3/16-mile (1.9 km) race. In 2007, a horse named Curlin finished first.

Good health has always been important to Marylanders. Baltimore is home to Johns Hopkins University and Johns Hopkins Hospital. The two places are known throughout the world as first-rate medical care and research facilities. In the 1800s, a man named John Hopkins made a lot of money as a grocer and railroad investor. A religious man, he wanted to use his money to help people. When he died in 1873, Hopkins left a lot of money to found a hospital and college.

From mountain biking in western Maryland (opposite) to studying at Johns Hopkins in Baltimore (above), people can find a challenge anywhere in the state.

Competitors race to see who can shuck 24 oysters the fastest at the National Oyster Shucking Championship.

Most of Maryland enjoys pleasant weather. Along the Eastern Shore, summers can be hot and humid, perfect for taking a dip in a stream or lake. Winters are usually mild. But snow can fall there, too. The Eastern Shore can get 8 to 10 inches (20–25 cm) a year. The mountains of western Maryland receive much more snow than that and stay cool even during the summer.

Many people take advantage of Maryland's fine weather to have fun at outdoor festivals. Each October, the St. Mary's County Oyster Festival is held in Leonardtown. During the National Oyster Shucking Championship, people from all over the country compete to see who can shell oysters the fastest and the best. Visitors can eat as many oysters as they want, shop at a flea market, watch a puppet show, or enjoy a hayride. Each June, at the Montgomery County Ethnic Heritage Festival near Silver Spring, people can eat foods and play games from 80 different countries.

YEAR

1967   Maryland's Thurgood Marshall becomes the first African American to serve on the U.S. Supreme Court.

EVENT

Ocean City, a popular scene for beachgoers, sits at Maryland's extreme eastern edge on the Atlantic Ocean.

Maryland and neighboring states begin working to clean up pollution in Chesapeake Bay.

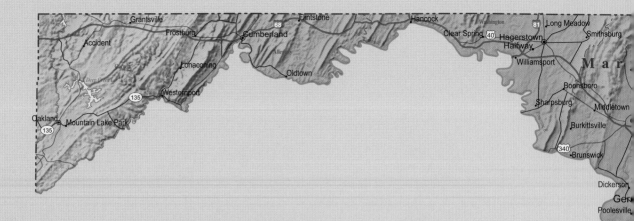

Maryland sports fans cheer for the National Football League's Baltimore Ravens and Major League Baseball's Baltimore Orioles. College sports also have many fans. The Native American game of lacrosse is popular among college students, especially since the University of Maryland ordinarily has a nationally ranked team.

Maryland has something to offer everyone. From hiking mountain trails to riding horses or digging for clams, visitors will never lack something to do. Every day, Maryland's ethnic neighborhoods, apple orchards, and bay waters provide a new and tasty experience for those willing to come and explore.

QUICK FACTS

Population: 5,615,727

Largest city: Baltimore (pop. 628,670)

Capital: Annapolis

Entered the union: April 28, 1788

Nickname: Old Line State

State flower: black-eyed Susan

State bird: Baltimore oriole

Size: 12,407 sq mi (32,134 sq km)—42nd-biggest in U.S.

Major industries: manufacturing, farming, fishing, tourism

BIBLIOGRAPHY

Larson, Kate Clifford. "Harriet Tubman Biography." Rpt. from *Bound for the Promised Land: Harriet Tubman, Portrait of an American Hero.* http://www.harriettubmanbiography.com/.

Maryland Office of Tourism. "Homepage." State of Maryland. http://www.mdisfun.org/.

Miller, Joanne. *Maryland & Delaware.* Emeryville, Calif.: Avalon Travel Publishing, 2001.

Office of the Secretary of State. "Maryland Kids Page." State of Maryland. http://www.mdkidspage.org/.

Rauth, Leslie. *Maryland.* New York: Benchmark Books, 2000.

Wanning, Esther. *Art of the State: Maryland.* New York: Henry N. Abrams, 1998.

INDEX